Better than Halloween

Better than Halloween

Bright alternatives for churches and children

Nick Harding

CHURCH HOUSE PUBLISHING

Church House Publishing
Church House
Great Smith Street
London SW1P 3NZ

Tel: 020 7898 1451
Fax: 020 7898 1449

ISBN-13 978-0-7151-4101-4
ISBN-10 0 7151 4101 5

Published 2006 by Church House Publishing

The opinions expressed in this book are those of the author and do not necessarily
reflect the official policy of the General Synod or The Archbishops' Council of the
Church of England.

Printed in England by Halstan & Co. Ltd, Amersham, Bucks.

Contents

Foreword

As a bishop, I am often asked what I think of trick-or-treat, or Halloween generally. As Halloween has become one of the great commercial success stories of the last few years, this question has come more frequently. Christian parents are rightly worried about possible connections between Halloween and various occult practices. Young people increasingly feel pressurized by their friends to join in with trick-or-treating, and the sale of Halloween-associated merchandise is now second only to Christmas decorations in the league of 'religious' festivals. Elderly people are also concerned about the increase in intimidation and violence connected with trick-or-treat calls.

I am not one for banning children from having fun. Christianity needs to make clear its positive message for young people – that Christ brings meaning and joy to their lives. And for many centuries there has been a positive Christian slant on Halloween. Eight hundred years ago the pagan autumn festival in Britain was christened *Halloween* – the holy night of blessing before All Saints' Day. I believe it is high time we reclaimed a Christian stake in this night. It can be a night of light and joy and hope, expressing the confidence we have in Christ who is the light of the world. So when I am asked, 'Should we ban Halloween for Christians?' My answer is 'No – let's re-christen Halloween!'

Better than Halloween will help us to do just that – it suggests approaches and ideas that are both biblical and child-centred. I hope that many more churches will take confidence from these, and begin a new wave of re-christening the occasion to become a positive opportunity for Christian outreach.

David Gillett
Bishop of Bolton

Introduction

It would be difficult to miss the hype and commercialization surrounding Halloween, 31 October. The media focus on it, and shops increasingly fill their shelves with items that are scary, frightening, and therefore very attractive to children. Many parents are willing to go along with all the trappings of Halloween by providing parties and encouraging the practice of trick-or-treat, but there are Christians and others who have concerns about aspects of the celebration.

There is a wide range of opinions on Halloween.

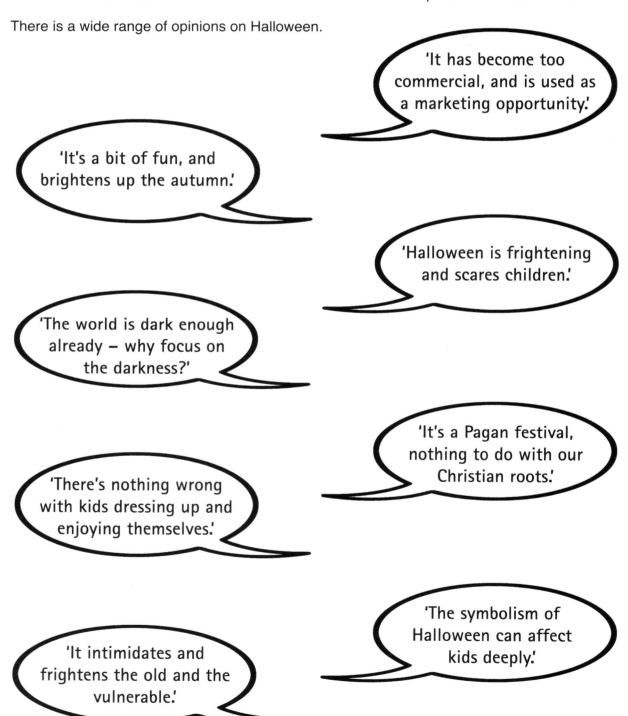

'It has become too commercial, and is used as a marketing opportunity.'

'It's a bit of fun, and brightens up the autumn.'

'Halloween is frightening and scares children.'

'The world is dark enough already – why focus on the darkness?'

'It's a Pagan festival, nothing to do with our Christian roots.'

'There's nothing wrong with kids dressing up and enjoying themselves.'

'The symbolism of Halloween can affect kids deeply.'

'It intimidates and frightens the old and the vulnerable.'

The purpose of this book is to help churches to look at the issues, learn where Halloween has come from, and do something about it by providing alternative activities. The book will give resources to the whole Church to reclaim the All Saints' celebration and to share the light of Christ in the community.

The book is in three sections.

Section One outlines the origins of Halloween and considers why Christians should not celebrate it. It gives reasons why Christians should try to reclaim Halloween as a celebration of the light of Christ.

Section Two provides all you will need for planning and running an alternative 'light' or 'bright' party for children on Halloween. It includes practical planning sheets, full guidance on child protection and health and safety issues, and suggestions for craft activities, talk outlines and songs.

Section Three includes the following supporting resources: fun sheets, posters, party invitations, a leaflet to be given to children, a pew leaflet for adult church members or to be given away on the doorstep, plus sheet music for original songs.

Most of these resources are also available in colour to be downloaded from the CD-ROM.

Additional sources of help and information are listed at the end of Section Three.

How to use the CD-ROM

Running the CD-ROM

Windows PC users:
The CD-ROM should start automatically. If you need to start the application manually, click on Start and select Run, then type d:\bth.exe (where d is the letter of your CD-ROM drive) and click on OK. The menu that appears gives you access to all the resources on the CD. No software is installed on to your computer.

Mac users:
The CD-ROM should start automatically. If you need to start the application manually, click on the CD icon on your desktop.

Viruses
We have checked the CD-ROM for viruses throughout its creation. However, you are advised to run your own virus-checking software over the CD-ROM before using it. Church House Publishing and The Archbishops' Council accepts no responsibility for damage or loss of data on your systems, however caused.

Copyright
The material on the CD-ROM is copyright © The Archbishops' Council 2006, unless otherwise specified. All industry trademarks are acknowledged. You are free to use this material within your own church or group, but the material must not be further distributed in any form without written permission from Church House Publishing. When using the resources from the CD-ROM please include the appropriate copyright notice.

Resources
The resources on the CD require Adobe Acrobat Reader for display and printing. If Acrobat Reader is already installed on your computer, it will be loaded automatically whenever required. If you do not have it, you can install Acrobat Reader by downloading the Reader from www.adobe.com. The 'Sample letter to the local press' and 'Sample text for a church or pew leaflet' are also available on the CD as word documents so that they can be adapted to your own situation.

Error messages
You may receive the error message, 'There is no application associated with the given file name extension.' If you are trying to read one of the resources, you should install the Adobe Acrobat Reader and try again.

Halloween traditions and history

The traditions associated with Halloween and their links with Druid and Celtic festivals are widely debated in books, in articles and on the Internet. There is little doubt that Halloween has roots in pre-Christian times, and it may also be a focus for present-day witches and Satanists. The traditions seem to draw on a number of sources, and the origins are therefore not clear-cut. But the debate rages on. . .

The name of the festival comes from 'All-Hallows' Eve', 1 November being identified by the Christian calendar as All Saints' Day. When Christianity spread throughout Britain the Church chose to adopt for some of its festivals dates that were already in use by the pagan Druids, and 1 November was the celebration of Samhain, lord of the dead. It was thought that on the evening before this celebration the barriers between life and death came down, and evil spirits roamed free. Celts lit bonfires, sang and danced in order to keep those souls away. The date also marked the beginning of winter and the start of the Druid year. But, despite the efforts of Pope Gregory IV in 835 – and of many others – to make and keep All Saints a Christian festival, the pagan elements of All Hallows' Eve have not gone away.

All Saints and All Souls

The Christian All Saints' Day on 1 November was and is a celebration of life, remembering both those who have served others and the Church in the past and Jesus himself, who brought light into the world to defeat fears and darkness. Sometimes known as All Hallows, meaning roughly 'All Holy People', it is a time to remember all the unnamed saints who do not have a saint's day of their own. The following day, All Souls, is sometimes called 'The Day of the Dead'. This is a day to remember all people who have died, whatever sort of lives they led. It is a happy occasion on which to think back on good times and to pray for the souls of those who have died.

Customs and traditions

The most obvious elements of Halloween, as it is celebrated in the USA, the UK and elsewhere, are based on various pagan rituals, some of which can be traced far back into the past.

Witches' masks and costumes are all linked with witchcraft, the occult, and Druid worship. There are those who argue that Halloween is the highest Satanic festival of the year, and who believe that under the cloak of the 'fun' aspects promoted to children the 'forces of darkness' are at work. Many others are concerned at the focus on a pre-Christian festival.

Other costumes (e.g. ghosts and monsters) are an important part of the modern Halloween celebration, and may also have pagan origins. Some think that, in order to be safe from the ghosts and evil spirits that roamed the earth on the feast of Samhain, it made sense to some people to dress up as ghosts or monsters themselves. Then the ghosts and monsters would think they were some of their own!

Pumpkins may be linked with witchcraft through the tradition of putting a candle in a skull to light the way to witchcraft meetings. The use of pumpkins themselves seems to be a relatively recent American addition – in the past, in the UK, turnips and other root vegetables were used for the same purpose.

The use of *lights and fire* is directly related to the Samhain celebration, as people lit fires to scare away the evil spirits. In more recent history the focus on fire has moved a few days into November, when on 5 November bonfires are lit to remember the Gunpowder Plot.

Feasts and parties were an integral part of the Samhain celebration, as the summer ended and the darkness of winter began. People thought that by being together and celebrating life they would keep the evil spirits at bay.

The *trick-or-treat* habit has a number of possible roots and is likely to be a combination of all of them. It may go back as far as the ninth-century Christian tradition of 'souling', when throughout Europe people would visit homes and offer to pray for the souls of those who had died, and in return would be given a cake.

In England there was a medieval 'Mischief Night' on 4 November, when young people would play tricks on others. The tradition of Mischief Night continues today in some parts of northern England, including Yorkshire.

In the USA, where the more recent rise in the popularity of Halloween originates, the trick-or-treat habit seems to date back to the early twentieth century, when a large group of Irish labourers threatened people on Halloween night in order to obtain money. This has since been toned down and is now seen in much of the United States as a light-hearted community activity.

Apple bobbing, the game where participants must pick apples from a tub of water using only their mouths, may date back to Roman times. The Romans celebrated the goddess of fruits and fruit-trees, named Pomona, at around the same time of year as the Druid Samhain. When the Romans came to Britain the game was absorbed into that celebration, and later into Halloween.

Halloween and Christians

There is a wide diversity of opinion on Halloween, both within the Church and in wider society (see p. vi). Many Christians and churches have a feeling that there is something inherently wrong about the celebration, but are unsure why it is not healthy, wholesome or positive. Others view it as a commercialized American import, and do not see any great harm in it. The differing stances are often backed by good arguments, but we have to face the reality of the situation: Halloween is growing and is no longer a Christian festival. As Christians we have a challenge in communicating our concerns to a world that does not take matters of spirituality – let alone occultism – seriously, or where a New Age 'anything goes' attitude prevails. Christians must avoid being seen as boring killjoys, yet should be clear about what may be dangerous or unwholesome.

So here are some reasons why Christians should reclaim Halloween:

Reclaiming our celebration

As Christians we are faced with alternatives: to ignore Halloween altogether; to go along with it without making any comment or protest; or to reclaim the festival for ourselves. As already discussed, the name Halloween comes from 'All Hallows' Eve' – the night before the Christian festival of All Hallows or All Saints, which since the eighth century has been celebrated on 1 November. It was the Christians who adopted the celebration of All Saints at the same time as the Celtic start of winter, based on the fact that through Jesus, the light of the world, all darkness is banished. All Saints should be and can be a celebration of good over evil, recognizing the power and authority of Jesus, surrounded by his saints and followers of all ages. We no longer live in a pagan age when occult and druidic practices dominate and have a place – we have been introduced to Christ, and our society should therefore be different. It is surely right that we stand up for the power and Lordship of Christ, and celebrate that rather than the secular and somewhat sinister myths of earlier generations.

Light is better!

There is certainly a morbid fascination in darkness, death and fear that is attractive to children. The young do need to know something of evil in order to understand that good also exists, and they must at times be exposed to death in order to understand that we are all physically mortal. There are those who would argue that Halloween is a good opportunity for children to be gently introduced to the darker side of life in an atmosphere of fun and celebration.

However, I would counter-argue that children are better served by having the realities of life and death carefully explained to them and dealt with when the opportunity arises, rather than by trivializing the power or strength of evil. Children live in a hard world, where there are many things that cause them pain and put them in danger. The society we have created is a difficult place for children, and there is enough darkness and evil to be going on with. Light is better for children.

We should take the opportunity to celebrate light: both the light and colour in the world that make it open, good and bright, and the light of Christ, who brings light to the dark places. The light of Christ shines on our world, helping children understand that Jesus cares about the darkness of pain and suffering, including that in their own lives.

Fear or love?

As Christians we should be thinking about what motivates us, and what we stand for in our world. We have the sprit of love and all the attributes associated with love that we read about in 1 Corinthians 13. Love conquers fear, and love defeats hatred and pain. The secularized

Halloween does not remember and celebrate those who have brought the love of Christ to the world in the past, but revels in fear and horror. While for many the 'fear' at Halloween is sanitized and shallow, for others Halloween is a reminder of the unknown and dark: the evil that we cannot see. It is not God's will that anyone should live their lives in fear, or that fear should be an element in the lives of Christ's followers. Why then support – or be ambivalent towards – a festival based on fear and horror, superstitions of an earlier age before the love of Christ was known and shared?

The problem with trick-or-treat

Many churches and communities in Britain are becoming increasingly concerned about the potential for anti-social behaviour and criminal activity under the cloak of trick-or-treat. For example, in Stoke-on-Trent the Saltbox Christian Centre has been very successful in leading campaigns against the practice, and has worked with the local education authority and the police in the process. It produces useful resources to help others to carry out similar local campaigns. (For contact details see the resources list at the end of Section Three.) While the background to the tradition may have had Christian roots in the custom of 'souling', the current practice is far from good or helpful.

In essence, trick-or-treat is demanding money with menaces, a practice which is a criminal offence and should not be condoned. While it may appear innocent to go around local streets ringing doorbells and asking people for sweets, treats or money, some people can feel scared or intimidated by the practice. Because of rising juvenile anti-social behaviour, householders can be put in fear of intimidation and of vandalism to their property if they refuse to 'play'. Each year there are many anecdotal accounts of windows, doors and cars being damaged and people being put in fear.

The practice of trick-or-treat also puts children in danger, even if they go around in small groups. Many parents who would normally keep a careful watch on what their children do and where they go allow children to wander around the streets, calling at strangers' homes and asking for things. Other adults accompany their children to keep them safe, a practice that can itself add to the intimidation felt by those put under pressure to offer a treat or face the consequences.

Those who criticize trick-or-treat are often condemned as killjoys who are stopping others having fun. But we need also to ask: who has the 'fun' in this context? Is it fun for the Christian who refuses to take part and is insulted and threatened by the adult with the child? Or for the elderly person who keeps answering the door to people dressed in frightening and bizarre costumes who demand that they hand things over or face a shocking trick? Community 'fun' must be for all people, not just for a few. This relatively new, imported element of Halloween is at best an irritating nuisance; at worst it becomes criminal harassment and extortion.

Cutting commercialism

In the USA Halloween is the second most popular public holiday, a huge amount of money being devoted to decorations, costumes and food. In the UK, as we have noted, Halloween seems to become more commercial every year. In addition, while large organized bonfire events around 5 November are still popular, there seems to be a decrease in families remembering the Gunpowder Plot by burning an effigy of Guido Fawkes. With the two celebrations being so close together more people are being drawn in by the commercial pressure of Halloween.

We must not fool ourselves – there is something attractive to children about witches' costumes and devil outfits, and it takes a supreme effort for parents to stick to a firm 'No' when trying to navigate children past the shelves and shelves of such items in supermarkets. In the same way that Christmas has been taken over by items and attractions that have nothing to do with Christ being born, so Halloween has been absorbed into our materialist world. The ever-increasing profile of Halloween puts pressure on individuals to go along with the crowd. Within that situation the truth of the light of Christ and the celebration of All Saints is lost, and the sinister and worrying aspects of Halloween are trivialized and hidden under cheap plastic horns and tacky outfits.

Celebrating the occult, Satan and evil

It could not be argued from any viewpoint that Halloween does not have origins in pre-Christian worship linked with the occult. The question that we must face as Christians is: does that matter? If we are clear that Christ is the light, then surely it can do no harm to us to see Halloween celebrated?

Yet the Bible is very clear about many areas of activity associated with the origins of Halloween, such as sorcery, witches, witchcraft, incantations and spells. It talks in vivid terms about the inability of good and evil to coexist and live in harmony and condemns those who underestimate or follow the evil one, Satan. Our concern is not only for those of us who live in the light of Christ, but for everyone who may come under evil influences, particularly children and the young.

There is an increasing interest in the occult, demonstrated by the popularity of books, films and computer games with storylines and examples of occult worship and practice. Through the internet information and help in learning about the occult is much more readily available, posing dangers similar to those we are more aware of concerning child abuse and grooming. Halloween is a danger to children and to others who dismiss it as a simple 'bit of fun', because it both trivializes the power of evil and distorts the truth. Halloween is in essence a celebration of evil over good; it can cause children to develop fears and become over-sensitive to the strength and influence of what we see as a defeated power. This distortion can manifest itself in fears of the dark, nightmares and horrific dreams, and a negative sense of their own vulnerability in a dangerous and dark world.

As Christians we may have concerns that children who are attracted to the darker side of Halloween will be drawn in to a fascination with the occult. The use of ouija boards and tarot cards is commonplace in many schools, leading children to play around with things that can become bigger and more sinister than they can cope with.

Ultimately, our view on this issue boils down to how we personally perceive the spiritual battle we are engaged in as Christians. There are a range of views within the Church, from those who see the devil around every corner at one extreme, to those who downplay biblical teachings about evil and question the existence of Satan at the other. The concern of many is that by condoning the Halloween celebrations, which hark back to a previous age and understanding, we open up the young – as well as adults – to unhelpful thoughts and ideas and deny our calling to share good news and to bring light into darkness.

What does the Bible say?

The Bible has plenty to say about many of the activities and images associated with the modern Halloween. These passages and summaries could be used in sessions with children, young people, youth groups, home groups and the whole Church to open up debate and consideration of what Halloween is all about. The leaflet master on pages 47–48 will also help to communicate concerns about Halloween.

There is no doubt that most of the occult practices we know today, along with fortune-telling, astrology and spiritualism, have been around at least since biblical times. These practices are condemned in the Bible, but never trivialized: the Bible writers make it clear that sorcery and divination in all its forms is real, dangerous, and not compatible with a life following God.

Some questions to consider alongside the Bible passages that follow:

■   Does the passage condemn the practice?

■   Does it trivialize the practice?

■   What does it have to say to us as followers of Christ?

■   What does it say about what we ignore, condone, or stand against?

2 Corinthians 6.16

> What agreement is there between the temple of God and idols? For we are the temple of the living God.

What we do about Halloween or other things in society that are so obviously against God's plan says a great deal about the people we are. If we join in – or even condone – Halloween, we are trying to have it all, but end up with nothing. As living temples we must be different.

Deuteronomy 18.10–11

> Let no one be found among you who sacrifices his son or daughter in the fire, who practises divination or sorcery, interprets omens, engages in witchcraft, or casts spells, or who is a medium or spiritist or who consults the dead.

This unequivocal passage highlights what God finds acceptable and unacceptable. There can be little doubt that Halloween traditions have their roots in many of the practices mentioned here, and it is alleged that Halloween is a prime time for people to engage in those activities.

This verse covers a number of issues, including the practice of child sacrifice in some primitive religions. It tells us to keep away from these activities.

Ephesians 6.11

Put on the full armour of God so that you can take your stand against the devil's schemes.

The clear suggestion here is that the devil is real, and that evil can influence us. We are to protect ourselves by trusting in God and making sure that we are strong enough to repel all evil. It may be easier to cast our worries about Halloween aside, but we are reminded that evil is real and that to underestimate its power is dangerous.

Acts 19.19

A number who had practised sorcery brought their scrolls together and burned them publicly. When they calculated the value of the scrolls, the total came to fifty thousand drachmas.

Those who converted to Christ and joined the growing ranks of the Early Church had to make a clear break with the things of the past. It is significant that the burning of sorcerers' scrolls is mentioned in particular, highlighting that destruction was the only way to be rid of these items, however high the cost. It would be wrong to keep them, to sell them, or to pass them on – they had to be destroyed.

Leviticus 19.31

Do not turn to mediums or seek out spiritists, for you will be defiled by them. I am the Lord your God.

The temptation, even for God's chosen people, to turn to others for guidance must have been prevalent for this rule in Leviticus to be written. It is made clear that not only is it wrong to turn to spiritists and those who claim to be able to tell the future, but it is damaging too. Being involved in these things means that spiritual damage is caused, and our spirits are defiled.

John 8.12

When Jesus spoke again to the people, he said, 'I am the light of the world. Whoever follows me will never walk in darkness, but will have the light of life.'

Jesus brings light into darkness, clarity to the confused, and right where there is wrong. Those of us who walk in the light of Christ should avoid all things that can lead us into darkness and help others to avoid them too. As Christians we can and should share that light with others, and bring light to the dark things of life.

SECTION TWO

Running a Bright Party

One of the most effective ways in which the Church can respond to Halloween is by providing an alternative party that focuses on light and gives children a really good time. The following section offers a guide to why and how to do it, along with a number of ideas and suggestions that should keep you going year after year. The theme for most of the activities is 'light', with a number of 'All Saints' suggestions also included.

Why run a special event?

Putting on a special event or party on Halloween is really important for the children in the church. They will be fully aware that their friends will be out and about doing trick-or-treat and dressing up, and will have seen the rows of Halloween materials on the shelves in local supermarkets. We rightly ask a lot of Christian children, who have to face a very hard world and must daily try to swim against the tide. Despite all the explaining and teaching we may do, children will still feel that they are missing out unless there is a quality alternative activity or event for them.

There may be some situations where the resources here can be used over a longer period, perhaps at after-school clubs or church-based midweek or Saturday groups. There may also be some value in mixing the 'Bright Party' ideas with the 'All Saints' suggestions.

A special event has a key mission element to it. There are parents outside the church who share some of the concerns and misgivings that we have about the rise and rise of Halloween, yet do not know how to stop their children jumping on the bandwagon. A local church with a good reputation offering an attractive event is an excellent way of reaching children and giving a clear, positive message to their families too.

Providing a Bright Party gives church children an opportunity to invite their friends along and share a little of their life and faith through it. Many children are skilled peer-evangelists and speak with disarming honesty to their friends about their beliefs; they need help in order to introduce their friends to the church.

The motivation behind providing an event such as this for children in the church and community helps church members to consider their attitude to Halloween and all that is associated with it. As well as being an opportunity to reach and protect children, it also provides an opening for adults to think through their attitudes.

There is something very important about making a clear Christian statement through a party or other special event for children. Gathering people together to think about bright colours, hear about the light of Christ, and sing songs of celebration and worship makes a spiritual difference to our churches and communities. On Halloween, of all nights, we should be clear about our commission to be lights in dark places, and to remember good people past and present.

Planning the event: Things to think through

Timing

The time you hold the party very much depends on the target age-group and whether Halloween falls midweek or at a weekend. (There is no evidence that Halloween falling on a Sunday reduces the trick-or-treat or other activities that take place.) To provide a positive alternative to tempting Halloween activities, it is best to hold the party in the evening – perhaps 6–8 or 7–9 p.m. – and to stick to 31 October if possible, even if that means changing service patterns for a day, or asking those who would normally use the church hall on that day to meet elsewhere. The ideas could also be used over a series, or on different dates, depending on when school half-term falls.

What to call your event

For this, anything goes! You may want to choose a name that makes clear that the event is about brightness and light; about good things and not bad; about having fun and not causing fear; or about saints, 'people of light', rather than ghouls. In choosing a name, consider all the possibilities given here, think of more, and check them out with adults and with children in the age range you hope to attract.

We have provided a few logos on page 11 to get you started.

Or try the following names:

Lights of the World Night	Bright and Light	Light Fantastic Party
All Saints' Celebration	Colour Crush	Fun under the Son
Amazing Light Night	We Love Light Night	Rainbow Party

Age range

Before planning in any great deal you need to decide what age range you are aiming at. The programme, activities and talk suggestions given in this book are aimed at a broad 5–11 age range: children who are currently at primary school. Teenagers need other activities to do and are likely to find some aspects of Halloween childish, but may have an increased interest in the more sinister aspects of the celebration. Under-fives are not as likely to understand the negative side of Halloween, and will not be able to attend evening events. Suggestions for teenagers and under-fives are on pages 19 and 20.

Programme

This sample programme could form a basis for any 'light' party, and is of course open to adaptation to suit your particular context. There are key elements which make this into a unique event which proclaims the light of Christ. This programme lasts two hours.

Sample timetable

−1.00 *Setting up.* Be in the venue in good time to get ready. Colourful drapes, blacked out windows, and coloured lights can make even the dullest church hall seem more interesting. Refreshments, craft activities, public address system and games all need setting up.

−10 *Registration.* Doors open and children are registered, using the sample form on page 15 or a form usually used by your church or denomination. If you have decided to split the children into groups, they need to be given a colour sticker at this point. There need to be a good number of adults to help parents and others fill in the registration forms; to show children where to go; and to run the games (see page 16 for advice on recommended numbers).

−10 *Active games* are provided. Play-canopy or parachute games are ideal for this, as they can be played with any number of children, so easily absorb additions as more children arrive.

05 *Together time.* By this stage most of the children will have arrived and registered. Worship, games and prayer could take place, with some simple and catchy songs that focus on the light of Christ, God's creation, colours, or saints (good people past and present).

30 *Craft activities.* Depending on numbers of children and activities provided, you may want to allow children to wander freely and do whatever they choose at this point, or to work in groups going from one thing to another. You could also build in an 'active' games alternative to provide time out for those children who work in short bursts!

1.15 *Food and drink.* This is a little more difficult than it was in the past, because of an increased awareness of allergies and food intolerance. Children love plenty of suitable food and drink — but don't underestimate how long it will take them to consume it!

1.40 *Together time.* Finish the party with some more stories, singing and interactive games.

2.00+ *Home time.* Make sure that all children are safely collected, and then clear up. It could take a while . . .

The planning sheet on page 13 will help you to ensure that you have thought of everything and have a team of helpers ready to fulfil their roles. By making clear all of the information here, and passing it on to all involved, confusion and last-minute panics can be avoided.

Planning sheet

.... Party, run by ....

.... Arrive and set up

.... Registration

.... Games

.... Together time ....

....

....

....

.... Craft activities ....

....

....

....

....

.... Refreshments

.... Together time ....

....

....

....

.... End

Where to hold your event

The venue you choose will depend on what will work in your situation. Schools are good resources, but some children may be put off. Churches can be inflexible, while village and community halls may be expensive to hire. The venue should be attractive and accessible, and able to withstand the rigour of children doing messy games and craft activities! You will also need a well-equipped kitchen and good washing facilities.

Health and safety issues

Make sure that the venue is safe, and that children are protected from any risks. Some of the basic risks include sharp corners on furniture, locked fire escapes, trailing electrical wires, and chairs stacked dangerously. Most churches have someone with some health and safety experience, who may be willing to look the venue over. Toilets need to be clean, at least adequate for the numbers, and if possible separated for adult and child use. They will need regular inspection by someone suitably checked through the CRB, who should avoid doing so when children are using the facilities.

Publicity

There are sample posters, party invitations and logos on the CD-ROM and in Section Three of this book for you to use or adapt to suit your situation. Where you send the publicity and how you promote the party will depend on your situation and your links with the local community. In a rural situation promotion of the event within a village school is likely to attract more children than in an urban area, where the links with the school may not be so strong. Response levels from among church children and families will be much higher than those from the community. Posters could be placed in windows, in shops and on community notice boards; and reduced in size and used as handouts in school and for Brownies, Cubs, and similar children's groups.

Bookings

It is always wise to have some form of booking before the event, so that you know how many children to cater for, how many to expect, and how many adults you will need in order to keep control and care of the children. Bookings could be made simply by calling a phone number and leaving a message, or by completing the full registration form. Inevitably there will be people who book but do not turn up, and others who turn up as the doors open. Even if you are able to accept children who simply turn up without booking, you will still need a responsible adult to fill in a registration form.

Registration

It is unwise to accept children who arrive on their own and do not have a registration form filled in. The adult that brings them must fill in a form before the child can stay. Check your church or denomination's child protection policy for details on this point. The form gives details of whom to contact in case of an emergency, and permission for help to be given in certain circumstances. It also provides useful information on any food which the child cannot have. Without a form you would be taking a considerable risk. Your church or denominational child protection policy may give more guidance on this.

Registration form

.... Party is being run by ....

Time ....

Date .... Venue ....

We are delighted to be able to provide a special event that has light and colours as the focus. To help us do our best for all the children who attend, please fill in this form.

Child's name ....

Address ....

Contact person and phone number during the event:

Name .... Phone number ....

Second contact person and number:

Name .... Phone number ....

Does your child have any special medical conditions?

Does your child have any food, drink or food colouring allergies?

Is there anything else we need to know?

Medical treatment: As the parent/legal guardian of the above-named person I agree to them receiving emergency medical treatment, including anaesthetic, as considered necessary by the medical authorities present.

I give my permission for my child to attend the party.

Signed .... Date ....

Relationship to child ....

Partnership

There is increasing evidence that it is not only Christian organizations and individuals who are worried about the unhelpful aspects of Halloween. There may therefore be possibilities for partnership with other local groups such as Cubs, Brownies, other clubs, and local organizations.

You may be able to involve Mothers' Union or Women's Institute members in providing the refreshments, to get a local firm to sponsor a gift for children to take home, or to ask a local school or college to provide some helpers for the craft activities.

Churches often struggle to provide adequate resources to run an event in glorious isolation, but if resources were pooled much more could be done. Certainly in smaller communities it would make sense to work through a 'Churches Together' or similar grouping in order to provide the best for the children and have the largest resource base of volunteers. In larger areas churches could combine and therefore hire a larger building, such as a leisure centre, in order to have a really big and well-organized party that attracts good numbers.

Team

You will need to ensure that you have a more than adequate number of adults involved as helpers and background workers. As a general rule, for an event such as this it is best to aim for a minimum ratio of one adult to every six children; having too many adults is better than having too few. You may prefer to allocate specific roles, such as those listed below:

Registration and keeping an eye on the toilets!

It is important that children get a warm welcome, but also that registration is run efficiently and quickly. There is also a need for a small team to make sure that toilets are clean and are not being used to play in. Child protection issues apply (see below). Depending on the area, there may also be a need for doorkeepers to keep out those who are too old or who may want to cause disruption.

Coordinator

Make sure that someone is in charge and has an overview of the organization and planning, as well as keeping the programme running on the night.

Refreshments team

The team needs to have a range of foods that are attractive to children and an ability to cope with children in a hurry!

Talks and Worship Leader/s

This could be the same person or two roles. Obviously, the people up-front need to be good communicators with children, and well organized, so that the main point of the evening is clearly communicated.

Craft team

Those delegated to run craft activities need to get hold of the necessary materials; they should set up well in advance, being prepared for energetic children.

Music group

Musicians will be needed to play the songs, although CDs will do if there is no possible alternative. The musicians need to practise, and to set up well in advance.

Child protection

As the party is likely to be for children without parents accompanying them, sensible child protection precautions need to be put in place. You should follow the policy of your church, denomination or diocese, making sure that all advice and guidelines are followed. You will need to ensure that any adults who may have unsupervised access to children during the event have an Enhanced Criminal Records Bureau (CRB) disclosure. Any additional adults who come along to help in the background (e.g. refreshments), who will be properly supervised and will not have unaccompanied access to children, do not necessarily need a check.

If parents opt to stay in the venue while the event is taking place they must have physical contact only with their own children. If you have any concerns about their behaviour you should speak to them, and if necessary ask them to leave.

Food

The basic rules for party food are: keep it simple and make sure there is plenty of it!

If there are cooking facilities, tinned hot-dog sausages are a popular option. Cold buffet food – sandwiches, crisps and cakes – is also popular. If possible, use some colouring, so that the food is attractive and matches the 'light and bright' theme. Do not provide nuts or nut-related products of any kind, and opt for fruit juices and water rather than fizzy drinks.

Costumes

Consider inviting children (and leaders and helpers too!) to dress up in bright, colourful costumes. Offering a prize for the most colourful person may be a useful added incentive. An alternative theme might be to dress up as good people from history. Make sure that your publicity makes clear that black outfits, witch and devil costumes, and the like are banned.

Give-aways

It is good to give children something to take away at the end of the party. Give items out as they leave rather than earlier; they could provide a distraction if given out too soon. Take-home items could include:

- Bookmarks (available to download from the resources section on the CD-ROM)

- Badges (you could use the graphics from the CD-ROM and follow the instructions provided there)

- Balloons

- Pens and crayons

- Books

- Toys

- Candles (but not matches!)

- Light sticks

- Models

Children will also take home any craft items they have made, once these are dry and safe to move.

Craft activities

There is a huge range of craft activities that will fit into a 'bright and light' or 'saints' theme, and are reasonably cheap to resource. If you choose messy craft activities, the information you send out should mention the need for an apron or old shirt. More details follow on page 20–23.

Games

There need to be a few active games, both to begin the session and as an option during the craft activities. There are a huge number of suitable games that can be played, some of which are listed below. It will help in preparing the event if you can find a suitable person to organize and lead all the games.

- parachute or play-canopy games: these can be borrowed from resource centres, denominational bases and schools

- relay games

- tag games

- dodge-ball (using large foam balls)

- leapfrog

- eating buns dangling on strings

- apple bobbing (see 'Customs and traditions' in Section One of this book)

Worship and talks

One of the key reasons for putting on a themed party is in order to communicate that Christians love colour, and that Jesus is the light of the world. Most children will enjoy singing lively and suitable praise and worship songs, and will listen attentively to well-communicated talks which include some elements of participation. We should not be ashamed of this element of the evening – this is the most important, and often the most effective part. However, these times should be fun, the talks short, the Bible communicated with life and vitality, and there is no need for formality. For suggested songs, chants and responses, and talk outlines, see the individual sections on these topics below.

Fun sheets

Fun sheets can provide either an option among all the other craft activities, or something for the children to take home. Some children will enjoy quietly working on these while others participate in the active games. Fun sheets linked with the suggested talk topics on pages 26–33 can be found in Section Three of this book.

Evaluation

It is important to get the views of children and of adult team-members during and after the event, to help in future planning. The coordinator should be observant throughout the party, and will have picked up on the stronger and weaker elements of the evening. To obtain feedback from children you could use a graffiti wall – a wall covered in paper for comments to be written on. The adult team may respond to a sheet asking for comments.

Follow-up

Some of the children who attend will not be in routine contact with the church. Through the registration forms you have contact details, which could be used to follow up those children and their families: for example, you might invite them to other special events and services (e.g. at Christmas). It is also important to encourage church children to keep in touch with others who attended – children are often the best people to invite other children to events.

Teenagers

A party of the kind suggested here is not likely to attract teenagers, who will find some of the input too young for them. But we need to recognize that young people are likely to have an interest in a broad range of spiritual things, and as occult themes are common in films, console games and books, some may be fascinated by Halloween and what it represents.

Options for teenagers include:

- Make sure that any church-based youth group looks at what the Bible has to say about occult issues and discusses them openly and honestly.

- Discuss with young people the socially negative aspects of Halloween, such as trick-or-treat, and ask them to think of the impact on all members of the community.

- Hold a special event for teenagers around the Halloween date, such as a 'grub-crawl' – going to different houses for each course of a meal.

- Have a sleep-over in church, with some worship and praise, prayer, teaching, games and fun activities focused on All Saints: all those who have gone before to light our way.

- Join with other youth groups in a wide area and hold an event, such as a quality band concert or good disco 'rave', which will also attract some non-church young people by invitation.

- Involve teenagers in the party for younger children, allocating to them roles such as running craft activities, leading games, or playing in a band.

Under-fives

Halloween is a difficult subject for children of this age, and many parents will not want their children to be scared by being told of the reality of good and evil. However, it may be appropriate to use the opportunities the church already has in place to communicate positive messages to younger children.

■ Focus on colour and light in the under-fives and crèche activities that take place in church, with suitable visual aids (balloons, paint, etc.) and songs.

■ Talk casually to parents about the negative side of Halloween at parent-and-toddler groups; try to discourage them from getting involved. Use some of the resources in this book and CD-ROM if appropriate (e.g. have some copies of the 'pew leaflet' or the take-away leaflet for children around, for those who want to understand why Christians are concerned about it). Encourage parents to give the money they would spend on costumes and parties to a local good cause.

■ Suggest that families spend the evening having a really good family time at home with a suitable video or DVD, and some food treats which make the children feel special.

Craft activities

These suggestions offer a range of craft activities with a 'light and colour', or a 'saints' theme (the latter indicated with an 'S'). Many of them require some specialist equipment or materials, which are available from craft shops and suppliers. If you have access to education supplier catalogues you may be able to find bulk quantities, offering considerable cost savings. Another source of some materials will be your local scrap store or play resource centre. These can be found in most areas; they are run for the benefit of playgroups and play-schemes by local councils and associated independent bodies.

Stained glass

There are stained-glass kits available, or you can easily do it yourself. Use permanent overhead projector pens and transparencies. It may be easier to pre-draw a design in thick black onto a transparency, which may then be photocopied for the children. The finished picture is best stuck to a window. The same could be done with thick black card outlines and coloured tissue paper.

Mobiles

This is another stained-glass suggestion. Once a shape has been decorated in different colours it can be cut out, a thin string attached, and hung onto windows.

Glass painting

Glass paints and cheap glasses are easily available. Make sure that children do not use too much paint, as it tends to run, and keep an eye on safety, as real glass is involved. Some glasses are the right shape to be used as nightlight holders – test them with a real nightlight first.

Glow tubes

Glow tubes are thin plastic tubes that glow in bright colours. They are available from craft and toy shops. They can be swung around, shaped, tied on wrists to become glowing bracelets, or can become hair-bands, and so on.

Friendship bracelets

Most children know how to weave a simple friendship bracelet using thread. Make sure that there is plenty of the most vividly coloured wool or thread available, and safety scissors that *will* actually cut!

Family trees (S)

This uses a small tree-branch for each child. Children draw members of their families, both living and gone, and hang the pictures on their 'tree'.

Scoobies®

These are lengths of plastic cord that have become popular over the last few years. They are available in toyshops and some clearance bookstores, and can be woven into bracelets. They are as popular with boys as with girls.

Parchments (S)

Beforehand, stain sheets of paper with tea and dry them. Using felt calligraphy pens, the children can then each write on their 'parchment' paper the names of people from the past and present who are 'saints' for them.

Friendly plastic®

Available from craft shops, 'friendly plastic' comes in strips of bright colours. Using hot-air guns, which need to be carefully supervised, the plastic can be shaped, engraved, and moulded to make patterns and shapes. Great fun, but best to practise it first.

Painting

Some children love painting. There are many things you could suggest connected with a bright and light theme, including rainbows, colours all around us, bright lights, and stars.

Card making (S)

There are many ways of making cards, the simplest being to fold up a sheet of A4 paper into a smaller card. Children could make a card wishing someone a 'Great All Saints', with a colourful design. Alternatively children could make cards for someone they rate highly, with the words 'You're a saint' on them.

Banner making

This is more of a corporate activity, and best suited to a situation where most of the children attending will be from church. Many churches hang banners, and by using plenty of fabric scraps in bright colours and fabric glue children could easily contribute to a big, colourful and bold banner. Themes could be 'Jesus, the light of the world'; 'We love light, we hate darkness'; 'Be bright with God!'; or 'We're All Saints!'. It would be best for someone to sew on the pieces of material after the event, as fabric glue tends to fail after a while. Fabric glue is available in many supermarkets.

Collage

In a similar way to the banners, a large, colourful collage can be contributed to by the children and displayed in church. This may be an incentive for children to come back to the church on a Sunday after the party.

Colour clothes

Spend some money in the local charity shops buying old clothes, and make sure you also have plenty of colourful fabric scraps. Using fabric glue, let the children stick bits of fabric onto the clothes to make fanciful, colourful outfits.

Tie-dye

Use cold-water dye. Twist T-shirts or pillow cases into 'sausages' and tie them up with string or elastic bands at about 5 cm intervals. Soak them in the dye solution according to the instructions, take out, unravel, and dry. With some dyes the colour can be sealed by adding salt.

Hand puppets

There are many ways to make hand puppets. One of the simplest is to use cheap gloves, make card or fabric faces, and stick them on to the gloves. There are many puppet-making books available with more complex designs.

T-shirt painting

Fabric paints are easily available, and can be used to personalize a T-shirt. However, paints are expensive and should be used carefully, as they run and blot easily.

Fimo®

This is coloured modelling material ideal for small items such as badges and brooches. With careful modelling really good designs can be made and then dried in an oven for a short time. Then badge-backs can be stuck on the back.

Mosaics

Plastic- and glass-based mosaic pieces are available from specialist craft suppliers. Mosaic pieces can be stuck onto small individual pieces of card by each child, or you could work on a larger design for all to contribute to.

Felt hats

Felt is easily available in all colours. Use thin card to make a hoop the size of a head, and cover it with one colour of felt. Then cut shapes from other bright felt and stick onto the hat using fabric glue or PVA, to make a really unique colourful fashion accessory.

Pizza making

If you have the facilities to cook food, then have a go at making colourful pizzas. You can buy pizza bases ready-made, on which to add lots of the usual ingredients that children love. You could also use a little food colouring to add shades. Make sure that you ensure good hygiene is in place for all those who handle food.

Smoothies

Colourful smoothies can be made using any combination of soft fruits, and enhanced by a drop of food colouring. Let the children decide what fruits to use, and allow them to make disgusting combinations – that's all part of the fun!

Paper marbling

You will need deep trays (like roasting tins) and marbling inks. Follow the instructions on the inks, using water, detergent and ink to make patterns on the paper. It is best laid flat to dry, as the ink runs if the paper is hung.

Scraperboard

Available from craft shops, scraperboards have layers of different colours underneath a top layer of black. Using sharp scrapers that are usually supplied with the boards, the layers are scraped through until the desired colours are found. Dramatic bright 'planets and stars' pictures can be created with a little practice.

Graffiti wall: Light

Have plenty of good wax crayons or thick felt pens available, and some thick layers of paper on the wall. Let the children write or draw on the paper anything to do with light and brightness.

Graffiti wall: All Saints (S)

The same materials are needed as for the previous activity. Let the children write the names – or draw the pictures – of any good people they know or have known.

Face painting

There are many face paints available. Sticks of colour are best if you want to be quick and not too detailed, but for artistic and careful designs liquid paints are best. A small number of children may have an allergy to face paints, so check first. You need to allow a minimum of three minutes for each child to have their face painted; always focus on bright themes.

Hair braids

Kits are easily available, and most girls will know what to do and will not want any help. In general boys will not want to do this!

Chants and responses

Children love learning simple responses to chants, and learn from the words as they say them. Here are some that could be used at the beginning of the party, or as part of the 'together times'. They are in no particular order, and may not all be suitable to every situation.

We don't want witches, tricks and fright

We hate darkness, we love light

We don't want to scare tonight

We hate darkness, we love light

We're into colours, we're into bright

We hate darkness, we love light

We love red, and orange, and white

We hate darkness, we love light

He came to tell of good things

Jesus is the light of the world

He came to make people well

Jesus is the light of the world

He came to get rid of the dark

Jesus is the light of the world

He came to change our lives

Jesus is the light of the world

We love the world, and all we see

We celebrate God's colours

We love the shades of green on trees

We celebrate God's colours

We love the red and blue of sky

We celebrate God's colours

We love the brightness in our lives

We celebrate God's colours

It's time to dress in colourful clothes

It's time for a bright celebration!

It's time for singing colourful songs

It's time for a bright celebration!

It's time for eating colourful food

It's time for a bright celebration!

It's time to think of our colourful God

It's time for a bright celebration!

We think of all the saints

We remember all good people

We think of those who suffered

We remember all good people

We think of those who were kind

We remember all good people

We think of those who brought light

We remember all good people

Bible passages

Using the Bible has great value, as long as it is communicated well and with energy. All these verses could be used in connection with 'light' and 'All Saints' themes. Ideally they could be learned by the children, with actions, and/or set to simple tunes.

- John 8.12 (NIV): Jesus . . . said, 'I am the light of the world.'

- 2 Corinthians 4.6 (GNB): 'Out of darkness the light shall shine!'

- 1 John 1.5 (GNB): God is light, and there is no darkness at all in him.

- Proverbs 13.9 (GNB): The righteous are like a light shining brightly.

- Romans 1.7 (NIV): Loved by God and called to be saints . . .

- Psalm 30.4 (NIV): Sing to the Lord, you saints of his!

Songs

There are some songs which touch upon the theme of light, and others which are simply good fun to sing with children at an event such as this. Don't worry too much about sticking to the theme – it is much better that the children have a great time praising God! Children who are part of the church community may know and enjoy some more 'adult' worship songs on the theme. Try to have a balance of faster and slower songs, and do not try to teach too many new ones. These suggestions may not suit your musicians or situation, in which case use some others and ignore this list!

- 'Lord, the light of your love is shining' (widely available)

- 'Light of the world, you stepped down' (widely available)

- 'Colours of day' (a popular song in schools)

- 'This little light of mine' (a fun song: *Kidsource*)

- 'I'm gonna shine' (children's song: *Kidsource*)

- 'Our God is a great big God' (a very popular children's song)

- 'We're a bright light together' (children's song: *Kidsource*)

- 'I am a lighthouse' (children's song: *Kidsource*)

- 'God's people' (children's song: *Kidsource*)

- 'Jesus is greater' (children's song: *Kidsource*)

- 'Like a candle flame' (a popular Christmas song)

For some new songs, see pages 49–51 in Section Three of this book.

Talks

The following talk suggestions are all in two parts, to be used during the two 'together times' suggested in the outline planning schedule above. They form the basis for talks and include illustrations where relevant; adapt and alter them to suit local styles and situations.

Opposites

Part 1

Illustration. Ask for a volunteer. Explain that you want him or her to say the opposite to all of the words you say. Then play the game until they run out of ideas or get one wrong. Make sure that the volunteer is thanked and given a gift for their trouble! You could repeat this with another volunteer if time allows.

Words you could use include: sad – happy; up – down; left – right; wet – dry; hard – soft; frown – smile; top – bottom; alive – dead; young – old; big – little; rich – poor; wide – narrow.

Talk points to cover:

- Close your eyes – it is probably not very dark.

- Imagine total darkness – no light anywhere.

- Dark and light are opposites.

- Dark reminds us of night.

- Who is (or was) afraid of the dark?

- A dark world, with lots of things that are bad.

- God does not like the world to be dark and painful.

- He sent Jesus to bring light into the world.

- How did Jesus bring light? (Healing, telling stories, giving hope, etc.)

- Jesus said a lot of things about himself.

- Jesus said, 'I am the light of the world.'

Part 2

Reminder. Ask the group to shout out some of the opposites from Part 1, above. Remind them that dark is the opposite of light.

Talk points to cover:

- If you went into a dark house you would put the light on.

- If you were outside in the dark you would use a torch.

- If you are dark inside you need light.

- Jesus is the light of the world, and the light for us.

- He wants us to shine, and he wants to shine in us.

- Jesus, the light, can make the darkness of sadness in us go away.

Illustration. Use trick candles that re-light themselves – but test them first, just in case they fail! Explain again that Jesus is the light, and Jesus' light will never go out. Light the candles and then blow them out – and watch in stunned amazement as they re-light.

Bright and light

Part 1

Illustration. Play a word-association game with two volunteers, who each in turn have to say a word to do with 'bright' or 'light', without repeating a word already used, and without hesitating.

During the talks, ask the children to make a star shape, by opening their hands quickly, every time you say 'bright' or 'light'.

Talk points to cover:

- In the beginning of the world everything was dark.

- God sent light to the world, so we could see all the good things he would make.

- The world at that time was really bright and light.

- The trees, flowers, animals, and everything were really bright.

- God was pleased with what he had made.

- But . . . when people came along, things started to go wrong.

- God told Adam and Eve, the first people, *not* to do something.

- Do you know what it was? Not to eat one kind of fruit.

- They disobeyed, and started to do wrong.

- The brightness wasn't so bright anymore, but God still loved them.

Part 2

Reminder. Ask three volunteers to stand in a row at the front and recap the story from earlier, each taking their turn to continue it.

Talk points to cover:

- For many, many years people made the world dark.

- What bad things did people do? (Wars, lies, anger, etc.)

- God wanted it to be light again, so he sent a special gift.

- A bright light showed three travellers the way to the gift.

- A bright crowd of angels told shepherds about the gift.

- What was that gift? (Jesus)

- The bright angels and bright light in the sky led the people.

- They went to see the light of the world, Jesus.

Colours of the rainbow

Part 1

Illustration. Ask another adult (a willing volunteer!) to help you with this, beforehand, and brief this person fully. Get this adult volunteer to come to the front, and then pour a full bucket of water all over them! (You may need to cover the floor before doing this; and it will be beneficial to your volunteer to use warm water.) The children will be stunned and excited by this! Remind them all that it would be very dull, cold, and horrible to be soaking wet all the time.

During the talk, ask the children to tap their hands gently whenever you mention 'water' or 'rain'.

Talk points to cover:

- The world was dirty, and God was washing it.

- People had made the world go wrong.

- Noah and his family got a boat ready.

- They filled it with animals.

- It rained . . . and rained . . . and rained . . . and rained . . .

- The water got higher.

- Finally the rain stopped, and the water went down.

- The world was a cleaner, brighter place.

- The sun shone down, and dried up the land.

- The animals ran off, adding colour to the whole world.

Part 2

Illustration. Get a paint colour chart from a local DIY store. Ask the children to guess what colour you are describing, from the name on the chart.

Talk points to cover:

- The animals ran off, adding colour to the world.

- Noah talked to God about how dull and hard the flood had been.

- God sent colours – in the form of a rainbow.

- God used the rainbow as a sign of his love for all people.

- God showed that he loves people, and he loves colours!

- When you see a rainbow, remember God's love.

Dazzling light

Part 1

Illustration. Ask for a volunteer to come to the front and have a blindfold put on. When this has been done, ask for one of the volunteer's friends to *quietly* come to the front. Get the blindfolded child to identify the other by touching their face.

Ask the group to hiss whenever you mention the name 'Saul'.

Talk points to cover:

- There was a man called Saul.

- Saul was clever, but didn't know that God loved him.

- Saul was not good, and did all he could to get at Christians.

- He had them arrested and sent to prison.

- He really hated Christians.

- Saul was going on a journey to arrest more Christians.

- He was blinded – by a really bright light.

- After the bright light he could not see anything.

Part 2

Reminder. Ask the children to shout out all together the answers to questions about the story so far, such as:

- The man's name was ....

- He really hated ....

- He saw a really bright ....

Talk points to cover:

- Saul saw a really bright light.

- He said it was a light 'much brighter than the sun'.

- While he was blinded by the light, Jesus spoke to him.

- Saul was completely changed.

- He changed his name to Paul, and his sight came back.

- He realized that the light was Jesus.

- Jesus is the light for us all – we can all meet him like Saul/Paul did.

The gift of colours

Part 1

Illustration. Ask for three volunteers to come to the front. Give each one 20 seconds to talk about what their best gift would be. Then ask a few of the other children to shout out what their best gift would be.

For this talk you will need a volunteer and a really bright coat or cloak.

Talk points to cover:

- There was a boy called Joseph, who had lots of brothers.

- He was given a really good gift by his dad.

- It wasn't a playstation or a game – it was a coat.

- The coat was fantastically colourful.

- It was the best, brightest coat anyone had ever had.

- Joseph's dad wanted him to know that he was special by giving him colours.

- Even though things got hard for Joseph, he never forgot the colourful coat.

Part 2

Illustration. Shout out a colour and ask the children to shout out anything they can think of that is that colour. Think of as many colours as you can.

Talk points to cover:

- Joseph's dad wanted him to have the best colours.

- God made us, and he is our father.

- God wants us to have the very best.

- That's why we have such bright colours in the world.

- God wants us to enjoy colour and light.

- He doesn't want us to get into darkness and dullness.

- God sent Jesus to bring light to the world.

Stephen, super-saint

Illustration. Invite two children to come out and answer a few questions about something that is important to them (football team, hobby, etc.). Then ask them what they would give up for their interest (money, time, etc).

Ask all the children to shout out 'Super-saint!' during this talk whenever you mention the name 'Stephen'.

Talk points to cover:

- Stephen had been around during Jesus' time.

- He decided that believing in Jesus was the most important thing to him.

- Stephen knew that being a Christian was dangerous.

- Stephen always spoke up for Jesus.

- Stephen was able to do amazing things through the power of Jesus.

- The religious people didn't like Stephen – they plotted to arrest him.

- Stephen carried on telling people about Jesus.

Part 2

Illustration. Ask two of the adult leaders to come to the front and play a simple trust game, by one of them falling back into the arms of the other. If appropriate, ask two (or more) children to come out and themselves repeat the game. Do make sure, though, that children who are to act as 'catchers' take their role seriously; and you and/or other adults should stand by to catch the 'trusting' child(ren), just in case.

Talk points to cover:

- Stephen trusted Jesus completely, even though he knew he was in danger.

- The religious leaders had him arrested.

- Stephen still spoke out for Jesus and did the right thing.

- The leaders hated him more, but he trusted Jesus.

- The leaders became so angry that they threw stones at Stephen.

- Stephen knew he was being attacked, but forgave those who were killing him.

- Stephen was really one of the first Saints who trusted Jesus.

Finish by asking the children to suggest what things about Stephen made him a saint. Suggestions may include trust, faith, determination, miracles, death, speaking out for Jesus, etc.

Saints for sure!

Part 1

Activity. Invite some of the adult helpers to the front, and ask each one in turn to finish the phrase 'A saint is…' Explain that many of us could be described as 'saints', and that we may have known people who seemed like saints to us, who have since died or moved away.

Talk points to cover:

- The Bible has many people who are 'saints'.

- Mary was Jesus' mother.

- She is a saint because she really cared about Jesus.

- She is a saint because she did what God said.

- Peter was one of Jesus' friends, the disciples.

- He is a saint because he always listened to Jesus.

- He is a saint because he was willing to learn.

Part 2

Illustration. Have a plastic sword available. Ask two children to tell you what they know about Saint George and act it out. If time allows, get other children to do the same.

Talk points to cover:

■ Saint George has many stories about him.

■ He is thought to have been killed for being a Christian around 1,750 years ago!

■ Saint George saved a whole village from starvation.

■ Saint George is thought to have saved a Princess from a dragon.

■ Why do you think he is called a saint?

■ There are many good people in the past and the present.

■ Good people could be thought of as being 'saints'.

Other possible talk themes

■ The brightness and glory of Solomon's temple

■ Moses and the burning bush

■ The pillar of fire leading the Israelites through the desert

■ Other leaders and saints from the Bible

■ The light of heaven as Jesus was baptized.

SECTION THREE

Resources

LIGHT SHEET

Opposites
Opposites

Fill in the faces

Happy   Sad

Dark things in my life ...
sad times

Dark things in the world ...

Wars

Jesus said ...

Connect the opposites

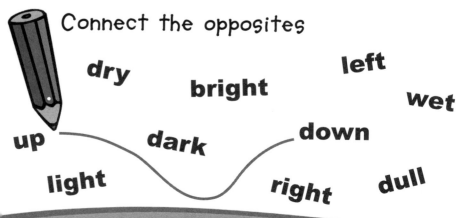

dry   left
bright   wet
up   dark   down
light   right   dull

I ____ the ____ of the

LIGHT SHEET

BRIGHT and **light**

Link the pictures with the story.

In the beginning there was darkness.

God made light.

God created many bright things.

Adam and Eve were made.

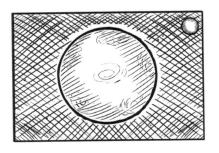

Find the words:

ANGELS **LIGHT** **STAR** **WAY**
GIFT **SHINE** **SKY** **BRIGHT**

B	A	S	H	I	N	E
S	N	R	G	A	S	B
T	G	I	F	T	E	R
W	E	B	P	E	S	I
A	L	I	G	H	T	G
Y	S	K	Y	E	A	H
O	M	C	F	N	R	T

Write the name of the light of the world.

– – – – –

COLOURS of the RAINBOW

Draw some pictures to finish Noah's photo album.

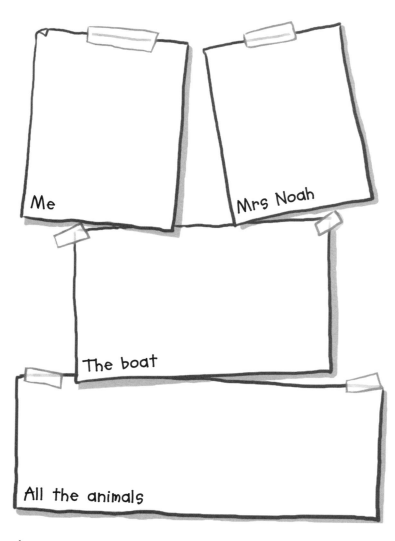

Me

Mrs Noah

The boat

All the animals

Good and bad things
tick ✓ the good
cross ✗ the bad

The world was messy

God sent a rainbow

The animals were safe

There was loads of rain

People had done bad things

God loves all people

Fill in God's message on the rainbow in the correct order:

love

all   I

people

LIGHT SHEET

DAZZLING LIGHT

What did Saul think before the dazzling light?

What did Paul think after the dazzling light?

Paul was known as Saul. He wanted to put _____ ✝ in _____ ▥. He was on his _____ 🚶 when he saw a _____ ✨ which made him blind.

Paul said the light was ...

Brighter than the _____

LIGHT SHEET

The gift of COLOURS

Ten bright things in the world God made:

_____

_____

_____

_____

_____

_____

_____

_____

What do you think the colourful coat looked like? Colour in the picture.

COLOUR IS GREAT!

Unravel the words and fill in the gaps!

Joseph was given a [gibthr] coat by his [dda].

He knew it was very [acpesli] but his brothers were

a [tib] jealous. The colours were [terga]!

SUPER-
SAINTS

Fill in what Stephen was thinking when he was in danger.

Circle the words that make someone a 'Super-Saint'.

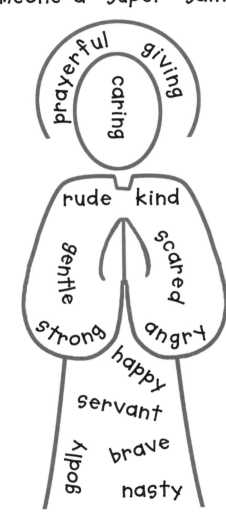

prayerful
giving
caring
rude
kind
gentle
scared
strong
angry
happy
servant
godly
brave
nasty

What did Stephen ask God to do to those who were attacking him? Colour the dotted sections.

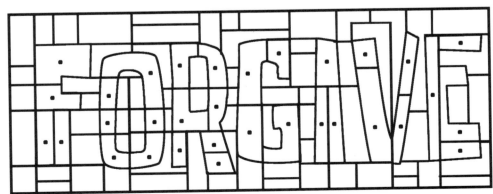

FORGIVE

ALL SAINTS

SUPER-SAINTS 2

Say this prayer:

> Loving God, thank you for all the saints.
>
> Help me to become one too. Amen.

Unravel the words and fill in the gaps!

Mary is a saint because

hes · · · · · · · drace · · · · · · rof · · · · · · · suJse

Peter is a saint because

eh · · · · · · · netiesld · · · · · · ot · · · · · · · suJse

GEORGE'S ORDER

Number the story in the correct order.

- [ ] The dragon eats the villagers' food.
- [ ] George kills the dragon.
- [ ] The people put food out for the dragon.
- [ ] George becomes a hero.
- [ ] A dragon lives in the hills.

My top ten 'Saints'

WE HATE
DARKNESS
WE LOVE
LIGHT
NO 'TRICK OR TREAT'
HERE THANK YOU!

We don't think that God wants us
to be into darkness and fear ...

FEAR

↓

fun

God wants us to
enjoy the light
and have fun!

OPPOSITES

BIG
↓
small

narrow
↓
wide

HIGH ↘ low

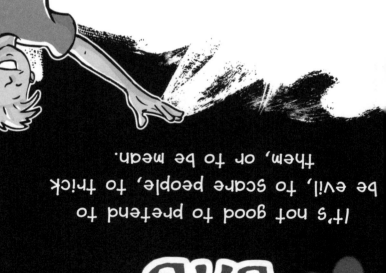

Instead of dressing
in black and doing dark
things, be bright and light.

LIGHT
↑
DARKNESS

Halloween has become a time of
fear and horror – it should
be the opposite.

It's not good to pretend to
be evil, to scare people, to trick
them, or to be mean.

BAD
↑
GOOD

Halloween used to be a happy time
to remember good people. Now it has
become the opposite.

BRIGHT and light PARTY

songs

food

.... Church

On ....

.... to ....

All children aged .... to .... welcome

crafts

fun activities

games

Contact ....for more details.
Bookings necessary.

Sample letter to the local press

Dear Editor,

At [insert name] Church we have become increasingly concerned about how people celebrate Halloween. We are worried about the safety of children doing trick-or-treat, and don't like the idea of people being scared or intimidated in their homes. As Christians we are also concerned about some of the more sinister and dark sides of Halloween.

We have decided to run a great new event for children on All Saints' Eve, or Halloween. It will celebrate brightness and light, with children invited to dress up in colourful clothes and think about the good things in life. There will be games and crafts, songs and great food. In this way we hope that a positive message may come through, rather than allowing children to be dragged down by darkness and fear.

The party is open to any children aged between [insert age] and [insert age] years.

For more details please contact [insert name and telephone number].

Sample text for a church or pew leaflet

Halloween and Christians

Halloween has become a major issue in the Church and in society, with a huge range of views. Many Christians and churches have a feeling that there is something inherently wrong about the celebration, but are unsure why it is not healthy, wholesome or positive. Christians do not want to be seen as boring killjoys, but we do want to be clear about what we see as dangerous or unwholesome.

Here are some reasons why Christians think Halloween should be 'reclaimed'.

Reclaiming our celebration

As Christians we are faced with alternatives: to ignore Halloween altogether; to go along with it without making any comment or protest; or to reclaim the festival for ourselves. The name 'Halloween' means 'All Hallows' Eve', as it marks the evening before All Hallows' or All Saints' Day, celebrated in the Christian calendar on 1 November. It was the Christians who adopted the celebration of All Saints at the same time as the Celtic start of winter, based on the fact that through Jesus, the light of the world, all darkness is banished. All Saints should be and can be a celebration of good over evil, recognizing the power and authority of Jesus, surrounded by his saints and followers in all ages.

Light is better!

There is certainly a morbid fascination in darkness, death and fear that is attractive to children. Many children live in a hard world, where there are many things that cause them pain and put them in danger. The society we have created is a difficult place for children, and there is enough darkness and evil to be going on with. We should take the opportunity to celebrate light: the light and colour in the world which makes it open, good and bright, but also the light of Christ, who brings light to the dark places. Light is better for children.

Fear or love?

As Christians we should be thinking about what motivates us, and what we stand for in our world. We have the spirit of love, and all the attributes associated with love that we read about in 1 Corinthians 13. Love conquers fear, and love defeats hatred and pain. Why then support or be ambivalent about a festival based on fear and horror, the superstitions of an earlier age, before the love of Christ was known and shared?

The problem with trick-or-treat

Many churches and communities in Britain are becoming increasingly concerned about the potential for anti-social behaviour and criminal activity under the cloak of trick-or-treat. While it may appear innocent to go round the local streets ringing doorbells and asking people for sweets, treats or money, some people can feel scared or intimidated by the practice.

The practice of trick-or-treat also puts children in danger, even if they go around in small groups. Many parents who would normally keep a careful watch on what their children do and where they go at this time allow their children to go wandering about the streets, calling at strangers' homes and asking for things.

Those who criticize trick-or-treat are often condemned as killjoys who are stopping people having fun. But we need to also ask: who has the 'fun' in this context? Is it fun for the those who refuse to take part? Is it fun for those who are intimidated?

Cutting commercialism

In the same way that Christmas has been taken over by items and attractions that have nothing to do with Christ being born, so Halloween has been absorbed into our materialist world. The ever-increasing profile of Halloween puts pressure on individuals to go along with the crowd, and within that the truth of the light of Christ and the celebration of All Saints is lost, and the sinister and worrying aspects of Halloween are trivialized and hidden under cheap plastic horns and tacky outfits.

Celebrating the occult, Satan and evil

It cannot be argued that Halloween does not have origins in pre-Christian worship linked with the occult. The question that we must face as Christians is: does that matter? The Bible is very clear about many areas of activity associated with the origins of Halloween, such as sorcery, witches, witchcraft, incantations and spells. It talks in vivid terms about the inability of good and evil to coexist or live in harmony, and condemns those who underestimate the evil one, Satan, or even follow him. Our concern is not only for those of us who live in the light of Christ, but for all people who may come under evil influences, and particularly for children and the young.

As Christians we may have some concerns that children who are attracted to the darker side of Halloween will be drawn in to a fascination with the occult. The use of ouija boards and tarot cards is commonplace in many schools; children play around with things that can become bigger and more sinister than they can cope with.

Ultimately this boils down to how we personally perceive the spiritual battle we are engaged in as Christians. There are different views in the church: from those who see the devil around every corner, at one extreme, to those who downplay biblical teachings about evil and question the existence of Satan, at the other. The concern of many is that by condoning the Halloween celebrations, which hark back to a previous age and understanding, we open up the young – as well as adults – to unhelpful thoughts and ideas, and deny our calling to share good news and bring light into darkness.

Shine Holy Light

There Are Saints

We All Love The Light

Resources list

Information about local campaigns and other resources:
Saltbox Leaflets, Gitana Street, Stoke-on-Trent, ST1 1DY
E-mail: tort@saltbox.org

Book of sessions and activities on 'Monster' themes:
Fright the Good Fright, published by Kevin Mayhew Ltd

Songbooks with songs for children:
Kidsource and *Kidsource 2*, published by Kevin Mayhew Ltd
Spring Harvest Kids Praise / Kids Praise party products

Video on the occult for use with teenagers:
Doorways to Danger, issued by the Reachout Trust.
E-mail: info@reachouttrust.org